THE

HISTORY AND PROGRESS OF SURGERY:

AN ADDRESS,

DELIVERED TO THE MEDICAL STUDENTS OF THE MELBOURNE HOSPITAL,
ON THE OCCASION OF THE PRESENTATION OF THE PRIZES IN
THE CLASS OF OPERATIVE SURGERY,

BY

JAMES GEORGE BEANEY, F.R.C.S.E.,

SENIOR SURGEON TO THE HOSPITAL.

MELBOURNE: F. F. BAILLIERE, PUBLISHER.
1877.

NOTE.

THIS Lecture was delivered on Friday, 14th December, 1877, in the Operating Theatre of the Melbourne Hospital, by Mr. JAMES GEORGE BEANEY, F.R.C.S.E., Senior Surgeon, on the occasion of the presentation of the gold and silver medals for proficiency in operative surgery, adjudged to certain of the students who attended his Lectures during the past session.

The presentations were made by Sir JOHN O'SHANASSY, K.C.M.G., as follows:—

GOLD MEDAL ...	... CHARLES JOHN TROOD.
FIRST SILVER MEDAL	... S. E. A. Z. WOINARSKI.
SECOND SILVER MEDAL	... THOS. R. LEWERS.
THIRD SILVER MEDAL	... E. G. OCHILTREE.

In presenting the medals, Sir James said—I have much pleasure in presenting you with these very valuable, and, no doubt, well-merited prizes from Dr. Beaney. I need not say that, as an old Victorian colonist, and one who stood upon the site of the Melbourne Hospital before the erection of the building was commenced, it affords me the greatest possible pleasure to be here on this occasion, and present the prizes which have been awarded by Dr. Beaney to the successful students, during the past year, in his class of operative surgery in connection with this institution. I think that scarcely anything can be regarded as more remarkable in the progress of the colony than the interesting event which has called us together to-day. You have before you a noble profession, and I have no doubt that you will be greatly encouraged in the pursuit of the studies necessary to thoroughly qualify you for that profession, by the fact of receiving these gold and silver medals from so eminent a surgeon as Dr.

Beaney, who has delighted us by the address which he has just read on "The History and Progress of Surgery."

In responding to a vote of thanks proposed by Dr. Beaney for his having acted as chairman, Sir JOHN said—Gentlemen, I thank you very much. I know no event in the past history of Victoria, the remembrance of which affords me greater gratification than the laying of the foundation-stone of the Melbourne Hospital. That took place in 1841, now thirty-six years ago. The year before the first stone of the Hospital was laid, the necessity for the establishment in this city of an institution for the relief of poor persons requiring surgical and medical aid became so apparent that a private house in Elizabeth-street was used for the purpose, under the management of a committee of benevolent gentlemen. The result of that small beginning is the Melbourne Hospital, a charitable institution of which the colony may well be proud, and the crowning glory of which,

I may say, is the Medical School that has been established in connection with it, where lectures on operative surgery are given by such competent men as Dr. Beaney and others on the honorary staff of the Hospital. I am very proud to have lived to see this day. To be present to-day has been one of the greatest pleasures that could possibly be afforded to me. I again thank you, Gentlemen, for the cordial vote of thanks which you have given me for presiding on this occasion.

THE HISTORY & PROGRESS OF SURGERY:

An Address,

DELIVERED TO THE STUDENTS OF THE MELBOURNE HOSPITAL, ON THE OCCASION OF THE PRESENTATION OF THE PRIZES IN THE CLASS OF OPERATIVE SURGERY,

BY JAMES GEORGE BEANEY, F.R.C.S.,

Senior Surgeon to the Hospital.

GENTLEMEN,

The science we study, the profession we pursue, is without contradiction one of the noblest and most beneficent that can occupy the attention of the human mind; and while in a mercantile and mercenary age it would be unwise to assert that we are indifferent to its substantial rewards, or that we despise the reputation which accompanies success, still I can confidently assert that every surgeon who is devoted to his calling finds in it a higher delight than one altogether independent of that which its emoluments and distinctions are capable of affording him. Viewed as a science, surgery presents itself to us in a twofold aspect: first, as subjecting to our scrutiny the structure of the most complex piece of living mechanism—the human body—to be met with in animated nature; and, secondly, by the minute and careful scrutiny of that body and each of its organs, both in health and disease, as furnishing us with the means of combating disease, of repairing injury, af assuaging pain, of remedying defect, of rectifying deformity, and of co-operating with nature in her restorative and conservative functions.

In so doing the surgeon may claim to be a public and private benefactor; and never more so than at the present time, when the wonderful discoveries of science have armed him with admirable instruments and with invaluable anæsthetics, which enable him to perform the most critical operations under circumstances calculated to inspire him with confidence and to exempt the patient to be operated upon from all suffering. When we look back upon the surgeons of only fifty years ago it must be candidly confessed that in spite of the highest skill, and the truest humanity, the operating-room *did* sometimes resemble a shamble, and that the reproach of butchery *did* occasionally apply to those who wielded the knife. But this was unavoidable; while there can be no doubt that it had the effect of stimulating experiment, of quickening invention, and of inducing the best surgeons of the day in all parts of the world to cast about for the means of pursuing their labours with improved appliances, so as to lessen the sum of individual suffering.

In reviewing the progress of surgical science during the last half century, precedence must be given to those anæsthetics, such as æther, chloroform, and the æther spray, which may be said to have revolutionized the practice of our art. By the discovery of these agents we are enabled to abolish the pain we should otherwise be compelled to inflict. It is said of Cheselden, the distinguished surgeon of the past, that on operating days he suffered great mental anguish at the thought of the awful amount of pain he was about to inflict on his fellow-creatures; but what a privilege is now entrusted to us—to be enabled to lay our patient for a time as if in death while he is undergoing some great surgical operation undertaken for the purpose of removing some dire disease or in reparation of the mutilations of injury.

Many of the operators of bygone days, unskilled in anatomy and pathology, are described as "agitated, trembling, miserable, hesitating in the midst of difficulties, turning round to their friends for that support which should come from within, feeling in the wound for things which they did not understand, holding consultations amid the cries of the patient, or even retiring to consult about his case, while he lay bleeding, in great pain and awful expectation." Now-a-days the operator is braced up with courage and calm composure as he gazes on his patient after the chloroform has "caused a deep sleep to fall upon him."

There is a common but exceedingly expressive phrase which has frequently been made use of, not merely with respect to great inventions, but to important reformatory improvements. People assert "the change was in the air," and this may be said with respect to the employment of æther as an anæsthetic, for the idea occurred, if not simultaneously, at any rate independently to many minds. It was foreshadowed upwards of 300 years ago by that illustrious French surgeon, Ambrose Paré, who must be regarded as the father of our modern science, and who was saved from the massacre of St. Bartholomew by the King himself, who sent for him into his own bedroom, and told him not to stir out, as he did not consider it to be right to murder a man who was so useful to the world. Paré, you know, put a stop to the barbarous practice of curing—or professing to cure—gunshot wounds by pouring boiling oil into them; and he also abolished the atrocious usage of cauterizing a limb to stop the hæmorrhage after amputation. An essentially humane operator, he was accustomed to produce local insensibility to pain by sustained pressure upon the nervous trunks leading to the part to be treated.

As far back as 1832 the young people of Athens, in the State of Georgia, were addicted to the inhalation of ether as a stimulant, but its first production of complete anæsthesia was the result of a practical joke. At a "quilting party" at Athens, in 1839, some boys and girls insisted upon a little "nigger" taking it "just for the fun of the thing." He fought furiously, then succumbed, and lay passive, breathing stertorously. They tried to arouse him, but could not. Becoming alarmed, a mounted messenger was

no small courage on the part of the late Sir James Simpson to advocate the use of anæsthetics in obstetrical cases. All the old hostility of religion to science was vehemently aroused; and a perfect storm of objurgation roared around his devoted head from pulpits innumerable. The Bible was ransacked for texts to prove that he was flying in the face of Providence.

Fiercely denunciatory sermons were preached against him, and he was told that to use chloroform was "to evade the primæval curse on women." But he was witty as he was brave and persevering, and he retorted on the clerical bigots thus:—"My opponents forget the 21st verse of the 2nd chapter of Genesis. That, said he, is the record of the first surgical operation ever performed, and that text proves that the Maker of the universe, before he took the rib from Adam's side, for the creation of Eve, caused a deep sleep to fall on Adam." It is said that when some of his clerical assailants read this brilliant retort in one of his pamphlets, they literally foamed at the mouth, and danced with rage. I do not wonder at it. They were blown to pieces by their own guns. After all, however, I am afraid we [illegible] modern invention. Most of [illegible] familiar with Iago's malicious [illegible] with respect to "the [illegible]

[illegible]

[illegible] mandragora,
[illegible] of the world,
[illegible] that sweet sleep
[illegible] yesterday."

[illegible] in the 24th chapter of his [illegible] that mandragora was adminis[illegible] administer chloroform. His words [illegible] He says: "It is given for [illegible] by serpents, and before incisions or [illegible] are made in the body, in order to insure [illegible] to the pain. *Indeed, for this last purpose, [illegible] the odour is quite sufficient to* [illegible]." Apuleius tells us that "by drinking [illegible] with wine, a limb may be cut off without any [illegible] of pain." An anæsthetic agent for producing insensibility to pain was in use among the [illegible] years ago; a preparation of Indian hemp for throwing the patient into a profound stupor was the agent employed. The anæsthetic properties of this plant were also known to the ancient Scythians.

Mesdric, a surgeon who flourished in the latter half of the thirteenth century, and who has left a curious work on surgery, alludes to what he calls "a flavour for performing surgical operations," composed of the following ingredients—"Opium, mulberry, henbane, mandrake, and lettuce, to be boiled until concentrated in a sponge, which when wanted was to be warmed, and applied to the nostrils of him who is to be operated on until he has fallen asleep, and so let the surgery be performed." Taking such facts as these into account, we can scarcely help acknowledging the fact of Solomon's deduction that "there is no new thing under the sun." Let us next glance at the invaluable instruments which the progress of scientific inquiry and of mechanical invention has placed in our hands of late years. In the discovery of the precise local seat of disease, or of the suspected accumulation of morbid matter, the use of the exploring needle is almost equivalent to the acquisition of another sense by the operative surgeon, as it penetrates beyond the range of his vision, and the reach of his touch; while it is so constructed as to admit of its being thrust with safety into the most vital parts of the body. Then, again, we have Carte's apparatus for the treatment of aneurism by compression. Less than a hundred years ago, when Dr. Wilmer published his "Cases in Surgery," there was not an instance of the successful performance of the operation for popliteal aneurism in the mother-country. Then came John Hunter's happy suggestion of tying the artery considerably above the tumour; then in case of femoral aneurism Abernethy's bold experiment of applying a ligature to the external iliac artery; then in cases of carotid aneurism, Dr. Mott's heroic method of tying the *arteria innominata*; and then the proceeding introduced by John Bell, of Edinburgh—that of tying the common carotid. Finally, if finality can be predicated of anything in surgery, we have the application of such a continuous compression of the trunk of an artery as either entirely interrupts the circulation, or diminishes it so materially, as to enable a sufficiency of blood clot to be deposited to occupy the entire sac. And it is interesting to observe how often distinguished writers of science have a kind of presentiment that certain discoveries will be made. Thus, Professor Porter, of Dublin, some years before the treatment of aneurism by compression was employed, remarked that "if there could be any other means devised for removing the impulse of the heart during the required period, a ligature never need be applied for the cure of aneurism." And when that means was hit upon, its simplicity was as remarkable as its efficacy; while the method of application cannot be better expressed than in the pithy advice of Professor Tufnell:—"Make your command over the circulation complete, but do so with the minimum amount of pressure by which this object can be gained."

No better attestation of the efficacy of compression as a cure for aneurism need be cited than the fact recorded in the *British and Foreign Medico-Chirurgical Review*, that in Dublin, during a period of eight years, compression was employed in thirty-nine cases, and in thirty out of them a complete cure was the gratifying result; whereas it is established on the best testimony, both at home and abroad, that one case out of three treated by ligature terminates fatally. Not only so, but the hospital records show that the average duration of a patient's stay in the hospital who is subjected to the treatment by ligature is twenty-five days longer than that of the inmate whose malady is dealt with by compression. The Edinburgh School of Surgery has been doing good service to suffering humanity of late by its successful treatment of aneurism by compression, and in England several cases of popliteal aneurism have been reported as *cured* by the simple application of Professor Esmarch's bloodless bandage.

Let me now call your attention, also, to what would have appeared in former ages the miraculous powers of the galvanic battery in restoring suspended animation, as well as for the treatment of muscular wasting and local paralysis: by its aid we can heat the cautery instantaneously—a matter of no ordinary importance in certain grave emergencies. It is fortunate that we are not living in the days of Pope Innocent III., who looked upon surgical operations as something diabolical: or in those of the Rev. Edward Massay, a Church of England clergyman, who in 1722 preached a sermon condemnatory of inoculation, and solemnly assured his awe-stricken hearers that Job's distemper was probably confluent small-pox, and that he had been doubtless inoculated by the devil. What would the great theologians who persecuted Albertus Magnus, who imprisoned Roger Bacon for seven years, who excommunicated Arnold de Villa Nova, who hunted to death the illustrious Vesalius, say—if they were now living and were still powerful—if they saw us with the galvanic battery apparently "creating a soul under the ribs of death?" Why, gentlemen, we should be in imminent risk of being burnt to death as sorcerers!

Dieulafoy's aspirator for drawing off purulent, serous, and other fluids without the introduction of air into the wound on the retraction of the perforating stilet is another inestimable boon to suffering humanity. We all know how, under the method introduced by Abernethy, in the case of chronic abscesses, for example, a part of the contents used to be drawn off by a trocar and canula, when the wound was allowed to heal by the first intention, when the puncture was repeated at fortnightly or longer intervals until the collection was so reduced in size as to admit of the cavity being laid open and healed from the bottom, like an ordinary abscess. We also know how great was the risk of inflammation under such circumstances, and that if any air was incautiously admitted into the wound it was apt to cause the putrefaction of the remaining matter, and thus set up a violent disturbance in the system. But now, with this aspirator in our hands, we can empty an abscess with the utmost facility and security, and give prompt and permanent relief to the patient.

Within the limits of a brief lecture it is impossible to do more than glance at Esmarch's bandage for bloodless operations; the spirometer, by which we measure the capacity of the chest; the urinometer, which enables us to test the specific gravity of the urine; Holt's urethral dilator, for the rapid cure of stricture of the urethra; and Weiss's instrument of a like character for cognate operations. By the former we accomplish, when skilfully handled, the forcible and instantaneous rupture of the contracted portion of the urethra; and experience justifies the assertion made by Sir Henry Thompson, that "by far the greater number of strictures, even of the most troublesome and obstinate forms, are quite amenable to carefully managed dilatation, either simple or continuous, and that it is very rarely incumbent on us to resort to operative procedures of any kind." And we all know the relief which this implies to the sufferers who come under our hands for treatment, and whom it is so desirable to exempt from unnecessary pain and inconvenience. Then there is that charming little instrument, the lithotrite, by the aid of which we can crush into fragments small stones within the bladder.

In speaking of instruments, however, I have perhaps been guilty of an oversight in not giving priority to the microscope; our very familiarity tends, I am afraid, to cause us to forget our enormous obligations to it. Without it, what should we have known of the mysteries of living structure, and of its marvellous functions? How could we have divined the primitive organisation of our vital tissues? The microscope does not enable us, and never can enable us, to fathom the mystery of mysteries—the origin of life—the invisible principle which animates the "monad" of Leibnitz, and the atom of Lucretius; but it shows us the earliest apparition of life as enveloped in visible form. It reveals to us in the blood vessels of our own bodies, the living substance out of which every particle of them is progressively built up and pulled to pieces again; while the uses of this instrument in disease are so innumerable, that to attempt to specify and illustrate them, would necessitate not merely an independent lecture, but a lengthy series of discourses. How the surgeons, anatomists, physiologists, and pathologists, of early days could have worked without it, is just as perplexing a problem as how the astronomers of primitive time could have explored the stellar universe without the aid of the telescope.

Optical science has also enriched that of surgery with the laryngoscope, which enables us to explore the recesses of the larynx, and to determine the exact position of small tumours, ulcers, and other morbid growths; to diagnose them with a precision and accuracy previously unattainable; to treat them by local application with a well grounded confidence of a successful result. It has also given us the ophthalmoscope, for which we are indebted to one of the greatest of living scientists, Professor Helmholtz, of Heidelberg, whose researches into the laws of sound, stamp him as one of the most brilliant experimentalists and investigators of the present age. By means of his admirable invention, we can [illegible] examine the optic nerve, retina, and choroid, either for observation or clinical demonstration; and note their appearance in health, and the morbid changes they undergo when subject to disease. And if I pass over the speculum, it is because we cannot claim it as a modern, much less as a recent invention, inasmuch as it was in use upwards of 1800 years ago, and some very good specimens of the instrument have been disentombed from the ruins of Pompeii. That beautiful little instrument the sphygmograph, for measuring the character and capacity of the pulse at the wrist and imprinting the same on paper is now extensively employed by the clinical physician, and by medical referees to insurance companies. The spirometer is also an invaluable instrument for testing the capacity of the pulmonary organs, and is much used by medical men both in public and private professional life.

Passing on to speak of new operations, one is oppressed by the magnitude of the field of invention and improvement which opens out before us as we review the scientific achievements of the last half century. If, in consequence of the artificial habits of society incidental to our complex civilization, the ease and luxury of modern life, the aggregation of vast masses of people in large cities, the increase of sedentary occupations, the growth of sensuality, and the morbid excitement and unhealthy stimulus which some or all of these cases communicate to the nervous system of men and women—but of women more particularly: if, I say, these circumstances have operated to multiply the number of organic diseases which afflict civilized mankind, surgical science, ever on the alert, ever active in the prosecution of its beneficent mission, has enabled us to grapple with these maladies, and thus to stem, if not to beat back, the advancing tide of human suffering. Twenty-seven years ago, the illustrious Lawrence asked whether the operation of ovariotomy could be "encouraged and continued without danger to the character of the profession?" But at this present time hundreds of lives are being annually saved by what has been justly pronounced to be "one of the greatest achievements of surgery in the nineteenth century;" and one which has also made its influence beneficially felt in every department of surgery. It was publicly stated a few years ago by the then Lord Chancellor, that by the first 500 operations for ovariotomy performed by Mr. Spencer Wells he had added something like 10,000 years to the lives of European women; and is is a gratifying fact, as mentioned by that gentleman in the address which he delivered before the British Medical Association at Manchester in August last, that out of 241 operations performed by his friend Dr. Thomas Keith, that skilful surgeon had succeeded in saving 206 lives. And if science is capable of effecting such brilliant results in regard to ovarian tumours, may we not confidently anticipate that it will be no less successful with respect to uterine tumours, especially in view of the fact that fibroid and fibro-cystic tumours of the uterus have already yielded to the hand of the surgeon?

The radical cure of reducible hernia by Wutzer, and which has been improved upon by Professor Wood, of King's College, London, is another remarkable gain for surgery. The method of drawing together the hernial apertures, so as to re-establish the valuable action of the inguinal canal, will, I doubt not, supersede earlier modes of treatment, and I share in the hope expressed by Mr. Spencer Wells, that we may yet succeed in obliterating the hernial sac, closing its abdominal orifice, and strengthening the abdominal walls by the use of insulated needles connected with the positive pole of a galvanic battery, causing shrinking and occlusion of the sac.

Of the various procedures for the cure of stricture by internal or external urethrotomy, it is almost unnecessary to speak; modern practice tends more and more to the substitution of carefully managed dilatation for the operative measures which were formerly resorted to, often at the cost of so much suffering to the patient, attended with serious risk of lacerating the organs, and bringing on hæmorrhage or local disturbance by the absorption of urine and pyæmia; and it is satisfactory to add, on the authority of Sir Henry Thompson, that in 219 cases of urethrotomy, carefully collected by himself from numerous operators, the deaths from all causes scarcely exceeded one per cent.

In the department of conservative surgery it would be difficult to over-estimate the value and importance of the operation of excising a diseased joint in preference to the amputation of the limb. How often in modern practice does it become our happy privilege to save a limb by resection of its joint, where half a century ago its sacrifice would have been rendered imperative? Not only so, but … the knife is now frequently obviated by … bination of the appliances of medicine … r, as I need scarcely remind you, … e sister sciences are more intimately … esent time than ever they were. To … s of an eminent member of our pro- … Miller, Professor of Surgery in the … Edinburgh, "the constitutional or … nt of wounds and sores, of bones and … ry affections, or spasms and pains, … more to advance true surgery in our … other agency whatever. Disease is … y and easily detected, and is more … ed; texture is better saved, function … y and thoroughly restored, and more victory is won, while the frame is less shaken in the struggle, and the opprobria of our art—its operations—are in consequence being limited within an ever-narrowing circle." These, gentlemen, are the triumphs not merely of science but of humanity; our skill becomes a benefaction; our experience a boon to our fellow-men; and the surgeon, instead of being regarded, as he was formerly, with something of the awe and dread investing one who carried about with him in great emergencies the whole armoury of formidable instruments of torture and mutilation, is now welcomed more frequently as the kindly and potent enemy of pain, and the invincible enemy of deformity and suffering.

For obvious reasons I refrain from doing more than making a passing allusion to new operations in surgery with which I have myself been identified; but I might be accused of mock modesty if I were to be altogether silent concerning the removal of the tongue by the wire cautery, and my operation for the radical cure of varicocele, which many of you have seen me do repeatedly and successfully. The application of tracheotomy to the extraction of foreign bodies from the windpipe and its use in dangerous cases of laryngismus; the relief of chronic affections of the female breast by hydrostatic or ærostatic pressure; the evacuation of abscesses from the tonsils by simple ablation; the feeding of patients through the nose and per anum, when they are unable to take sustenance by the ordinary channel; the reparation or restoration of the nose by the methods introduced by Liston and Diefenbach; the twisting of arteries instead of tying them; the reduction of dislocations by simple manipulation in lieu of pullies; the immense improvements which have taken place in lithotomy; the simplified cure of hydrocele by the injection of iodine; the cure of fungoid testicle without the use of the knife; the removal of hæmorrhoids by excision and cautery; the application of the principle of subcutaneous section to the elimination of loose cartilages in joints; the reformed treatment of wounds and sores by simple water dressing; carbolic acid, and other valuable and economical antiseptics; by better attention to position, and by the use of plaster of Paris and dextrine bandages.

These, gentlemen, are a few only of the improvements in the practice of surgery, which have been effected during the last half century. I should only weary your patience if I entered into fuller details concerning them. But ours is a science in which we are ever learning; and in which the progress of discovery is virtually unlimited. It is with surgery, as with one of the athletic pastimes of classical antiquity, each generation transmits to the next the light it has acquired from observation, from study, from experiment and practice—

> "As though a torch-race, where from hand to hand,
> The flying youths transmit their shining brand."

A new surgical operation may be the means of saving the life of a great warrior, statesman, orator, artist, author, or man of science, whose loss would be an irreparable calamity to his own nation, and possibly to mankind, while professional ignorance, and a blind adherence to the superstitious errors of the past, may on the other hand, send to an early grave one who—

> "Became on fortune's crowning slope,
> The pillar of a people's hope,
> The centre of a world's desire."

Nay more, the safety of a nation may depend upon something so simple, and apparently so insignificant as the prompt use of a commonplace surgical instrument, of which we have a curious illustration in an incident which occurred shortly after the foundation of the colony at New Plymouth in North America:—Edward Winslow, one of the first settlers, heard that Massasut, an Indian chief, was sick and like to die; he found him with a houseful of people about him; women rubbing his arms and legs, and friends making such a hellish noise as they probably thought would scare away the devil of sickness. Winslow gave him some conserve, washed his mouth, scraped his tongue, which was in a horrid state; got down some drink, made him some broth, dosed him with an infusion of strawberry leaves and sassafras root, and had the satisfaction of seeing him recover. Massasut, full of gratitude, revealed the plot that had been formed to destroy the colonists, whereupon the Governor ordered Captain Miles Standish to see to them, who thereupon stabbed Picksnot with his own knife, broke up the plot, saved the colony; and thus—as Dr. Holmes says, who related the story, "rendered Massachusetts and the Massachusetts Medical Society a possibility, as they now are a fact before us."

In conclusion, suffer me to remind you that ours is both an art and a science! an art in so far as it involves the performance of the various manual duties required, or the employment of the means invented for us by the skilful mechanist, and a science in relation to the choice and application of such means. Both the art and science must

[illegible]

... you had least reason to expect it. So on the other hand, you will find your patient sink into the grave when you thought you had a fair prospect of success.

I have now operated," he adds, "twenty-seven times, and have lost five cases; I have taken every case that has presented itself without shrinking." Brave words these, gentlemen, and worthy to be borne in remembrance by all of us in the practice of a profession where each may lay to heart the sound advice offered to Laertes by Polonius:—

> "To thine own self be true:
> And it must follow, as the night the day,
> Thou canst not then be false to any man.
> Farewell; my blessing season this in thee."

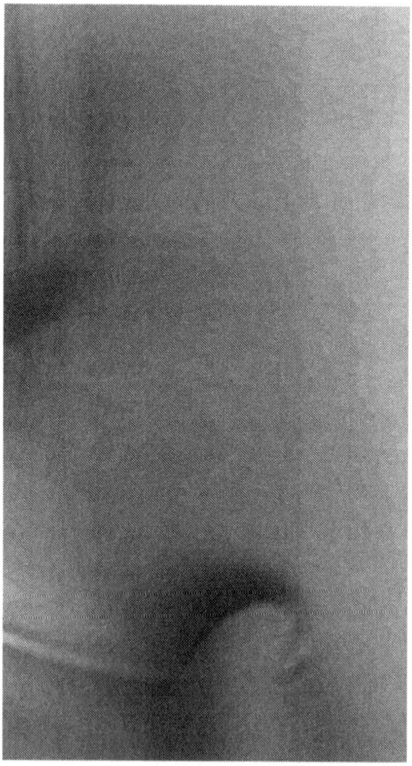

Milton Keynes UK
Ingram Content Group UK Ltd.
UKHW021437290424
441933UK00030B/309

9 781018 150543

As near a *facsimile* of the original as possible

A NARRATIVE

OF

A LIGHT COMPANY SOLDIER'S SERVICE,

IN

THE 41st REGIMENT OF FOOT,

DURING THE LATE

AMERICAN WAR;

TOGETHER

WITH SOME ADVENTURES

AMONGST

THE INDIAN TRIBES,

FROM 1812 TO 1814.

BRADFORD
PRINTED AND PUBLISHED BY JOHN BUBB,
AND SOLD BY THE AUTHOR

Price One Shilling.

1840.

EDITOR'S PREFACE

SO far as investigation has shown, there is but a single copy known of the *Narrative* of Shadrach Byfield; and even this has only come to light within three years. It is from this original, now owned by Mr. Wilberforce Eames, and by his permission that our present edition is made.

The style is so good as to make it tolerably certain that the soldier (who acknowledges himself to have neglected educational opportunities) enjoyed the advantage of a more skilled amanuensis; but it is occasionally relieved by a phrase of pure Doric, stamping it with the hall-mark of genuine rustic English.

As a contribution to the scanty literature of the War of 1812 it possesses much positive value, particularly in its details regarding the Indian allies of the British. While one or two references to the same facts are to be found in letters of British officers, nothing from a private soldier has heretofore been known to exist; and his revelation of the savages' atrocities is of genuine historical interest.

His vivid account of the various actions in which he shared leaves little to be desired; and though but one of those whom Napier describes in his ***Peninsular War*** as "conquering under the cool shade of aristocracy, no honors awaiting his daring, his life of danger and hardship uncheered by hope"—it is evident both from his story and his being one of the light-infantry (the best men of each regiment) that he was considerably above the average private in intelligence.

That one of our own writers who has seen fit to sneer at 1812 as "an opera-bouffé war" might well read the simple statement of Byfield's company, reduced from 110 men to 15 by death, wounds and capture.

Such losses do not point to Scott, Pike, Ripley and their men as carrying on anything but war in deadly earnest.

EDITOR.

A NARRATIVE

&c., &c.,

I WAS born at Woolley, near Bradford, in the county of Wilts, on the 16th day of September, 1789, the same day on which his Majesty King George the Third came from Longleat to Trowbridge. I entered the Militia service in the year 1807. My mother on hearing I was enlisted (and having two sons before in the army) was so affected that on the evening of the same day she fell in a fit and never spoke after, and I was obliged to march off the next morning; she expired on the third day after. Our route was for Newcastle upon Tyne, where I joined the Wiltshire regiment of Militia.

After I had learned my discipline the regiment marched to Norman Cross, to do duty over French prisoners. Those of us who were not perfect in our duty were detached to Petersburgh for improvement; myself with others were soon returned to prison, being considered fit for duty. Our next route was for Ipswich (Suffolk); I then got a furlough to go home to see my friends. After returning to my regiment an order was given for volunteering to the line; a considerable number volunteered to the 41st foot, and having a brother in that corps I was one of the number: the volunteers soon marched for Portsmouth, and from thence to the Isle of Wight, in May, 1809, embarked on board the *Robert* transport, and sailed for Quebec; we had a good passage, and arrived in about nine or ten weeks. While at anchor off Quebec we received orders to take boats and go up the river St. Lawrence; a few miles up the river an aide-de-camp from the beach communicated counter-orders, and we returned to Quebec and occupied (the) Jesuits' barracks. After having been there some time, a sergeant came into the barrack-room and asked if there was a lad who wished to be groom to the Quartermaster-General; I replied that I would go. Having dressed myself the sergeant took me to the Quartermaster-General, who asked me if I understood looking after horses; I said I did not, but that I was willing to learn. He replied, "You are the lad, I do not want one that knows too much"; he appeared to take an interest in me, as he used to come himself and instruct me in cleaning the horses, &c., and ordered me to Lower Town, to be measured for two suits of clothes. In the winter he went to Montreal and took me with him, and understanding that I had a brother in the 41st, asked me if I should like to see him, as the regiment was expected at Montreal; he gave me leave to wait his arrival, after which I was to return to Quebec without him, as he was going into the States for a short time. While in company with my brother Colonel Proctor[1] enquired who I was, I being dressed in coloured clothes,[2] he was told I was one of the volunteers come out to join the regiment; he ordered me into the barracks, where I received a suit of regimentals and was ordered into the ranks. I felt very much hurt at being taken away from my master without his knowledge. When he returned from the States to Montreal, and finding that I was not gone to Quebec, he sent to the barracks for me. I waited on him and he asked me why I had not returned to Quebec; I told him the reason and asked if he would wait on the colonel to get me leave to go with him. He said he should not humble (himself) to the colonel, but the clothes and the money he gave me I was to keep. I was then put into the same company my brother was in (Captain Crowder's †). I had not joined the company long when my captain asked me if I was a scholar, and when I told him I was not, he wished me to go to

[1]This was Henry Proctor, Lieut Colonel of the 41st, whom we shall meet again. His record during the war of 1812 is part of history He became a brigadier general but proved unworthy of the promotion.

[2] Civilian clothes is meant.

† William L. Crowther.

school, and said that he would make a non-commissioned officer of me; which offer I refused, being young and foolish Some time after this I was picked out for the light infantry company (Captain Muir's *). Soon after the flank companies received orders to go to Quebec, to form light and heavy brigades, where I had the pleasure of seeing my old master, who treated me very kindly; the brigade was broken up and we returned to Montreal. After lying there about a year and a half we received a route for Fort George.[3] While (t)here several incidents happened in which my life was wonderfully preserved. One day while standing on the quay, a sergeant who was ordered to York [4] on command, when going on board his sword fell from its scabbard into the water. I heard him lamenting about it very much, and being a good swimmer I undressed, went into the water and dived for it, found it and brought it up. The sergeant was very thankful and offered me anything I would accept; but this act produced a fit of illness (I being under water a considerable time) and it affected my head. Soon after my recovery, as we were on a fishing party, I was employed in holding one end of the net; and with the violence of the wind and the waves I was pulled into the water from the ice on which I was standing, and came into contact with the boat and was almost squeezed to death between the boat and the ice. I was pulled into the boat and carried to the barracks, very much bruised, but no bones were broken. Soon after this we heard that war was proclaimed between England and America.

One Sunday morning, being on sentry on the bank of the river St. Lawrence, I saw a boat drifting down the river, without any person in it; a party of men was warned to go and bring in the boat. While the men were out, the Americans fired on them, which

* Adam Muir

[3] Opposite Youngstown, N Y., and about seven miles north of Queenstown, Canada

[4] Now Toronto.

was the first shot I saw fired in anger. On their return General Brock[5] being informed of the transaction ordered them out immediately, to bring in the boat, and said if they fired again he would open the batteries upon them; they went out and brought her in without any further firing. The General immediately gave orders for a large bank to be thrown up, in front of the American fort, to preserve the town. Every man went to work immediately, the General staying with us all night. As the flank companies did the duty at the Government House, I was amongst them. Our general was very much beloved; he used to come out and talk familiarly with us. After fortifying the town, we understood the Americans had crossed the river from Detroit to Sandwich, to which place we were ordered to march.

We proceeded to Oxford and collected as many volunteers as we could, and from thence to Long Point, where General Brock met us with reinforcements. We then went on to Malden. The general there gave orders for every man that was fit for duty to march for Sandwich, and we left Malden under his command. The Americans had erected works at Sandwich, but hearing that we were advancing, they burnt and destroyed them, and returned over to Detroit. When we arrived at Sandwich the general gave orders to build batteries opposite the town and fort of Detroit. When the works were completed, which was on Sunday morning, August 16, 1812, orders were given for the batteries to be opened, and about five hundred of the troops, besides a few Indians and volunteers, were ordered to cross the river in boats, below Sandwich: our general was with us; we made our landing good and marched towards the town. When we entered the field in front of the American fort we were marched rank and file, and halted; the enemy at the same time marched out of the fort and formed in three columns; after a short time they returned into the fort again.

[5] Afterwards Sir Isaac, major-general and lieutenant-colonel of the 49th Foot, killed at the battle of Queenstown, October 13, 1812.

Our general gave orders that all the spare jackets were to be given to the volunteers, and extended the lines as far as possible. After awhile an officer came from the fort with a flag of truce: General Brock came up to meet the flag of truce, with his attendants to the advance. I was on the advance with the general at the time, and from what we could hear the officer wanted three days' cessation; to which our general replied if they did not yield in three hours, he would blow up every one of them. The officer went back with this message, and returned very soon, with an authority to surrender the fort; the enemy shortly after marched out of the fort and laid down their arms, and we marched in. There was a party warned (of which I was one) to go through the fort, to see if any of the enemy were remaining in it, when I saw three American officers lying dead. One of the men told that one of the officers (had) said, before night he would wash his hands in British blood. We found two or three of the enemy remaining in the officers' apartments; they were about to destroy the colors of the 4th American regiment, but we took the colours from them. Entering another room, I saw several men and ordered them out. Whilst walking along I slipped and nearly fell; one of the men said, "My dear man, that is the brains of a man killed with one of our shots." After we had got possession, and the prisoners were sent off, our general, who was about to leave us, assembled the troops and thanked them for their gallantry, saying it would be a feather in our caps as long as we lived Orders were then given to fire off the Americans' arms. After discharging many of them, we were obliged to leave off and draw the charges, as they were so heavily loaded, some with a musket ball and nine buckshots. But notwithstanding I thus shared in the dangers of the capture, I have received no share of the prize-money. Two different payments have been made for Detroit, amounting to several pounds each man, but I have received neither; owing to the neglect of the clerk or some other cause my name was omitted from being inserted in the prize-list.

After this news was received that the Indians had surrounded an American fort. About two hundred of us, under the command of Captain Muir, were ordered to march towards the Mawme[6] Rapids. We encamped for several days; we then received orders to march to Fort Defiance.[7] Part of us marched through the woods, the others, with the ammunition and provisions went up the Mawme river in boats. We halted one night, the next morning crossed the river and marched on through the woods until we came to a large open space, where we camped. In the evening Lieutenant Barnett came to us and asked us for some provisions, as he had tasted none all the day. We being scarce, my comrade asked me what he was to do. I told him to give him some, as he was a gentleman and a soldier.

In the night we were alarmed by an Indian whoop; every man was instantly ordered to stand to his arms. In a short time six Indians and an interpreter entered the camp, who informed the captain that they had been out as spies, and in the evening, whilst passing through the woods, they saw a light and made towards it. On arriving near they discovered five Americans surrounding a fire; they drew near, and when the Americans saw them they ran to their arms. They (the Indians) ordered them to give them up immediately One of the Americans, who was an officer, asked if they had any British soldiers in camp. They replied "No." He then said, "We will not go with you, but you shall come with us." The Indians immediately surrounded them and took them prisoners. While marching them, the officer was heard by the interpreter to say to the men, "Kill four of the Indians, and make your escape";

[6] Maumee

[7] At the junction of the Maumee and Auglaize rivers, fifty miles from Fort Wayne, Indiana.

upon which the interpreter ordered the Indians to kill four of the Americans, which they did; the officer endeavouring to escape, the interpreter shot him whilst running.† To convince our captain that what they related was true, they pulled from their girdles the five scalps, the officer's ears, and a silver-mounted dagger. We were then ordered to lie upon our arms, and in the morning we returned to Fort Defiance, crossed the river and encamped.

The next morning we heard an Indian whoop. Soon after the Indians brought in an American prisoner. The captain asked the prisoner who he was and how he was taken. He said he was a quartermaster-sergeant[8] of an American regiment, and was out hunting for honey The captain then asked him how many they had in camp, and how far they were off. He replied, about 9000, and that they intended to camp there to-night, but that it was doubtful, as they had to cut the road through the wood for the cannon. Captain Muir then said to Captain Elliott[9] (commanding the Indians), "We had better retreat as quickly as possible" Captain Elliott replied, he would rather an attempt might be made to cut off their advance. Our captain answered, "If we are exposed to one volley I shall lose all my men, therefore I think it advisable to retreat," to which Captain Elliott agreed. We then lightened the boats, by throwing the shot overboard, and retreated to Malden.

After this we were again sent to the Mawme Rapids, with two

† This was the Indians' story; the facts are that the party consisted of Ensign Leggett, 17th U. S. Infantry, and four privates of a Woodford (Ky.) volunteer company The probability is that the unfortunate squad were surprised while asleep, and all murdered.

[8] The sergeant was —— McCoy, of the regiment commanded by Gov. Charles Scott, of Kentucky History records that his shrewd reply caused Muir's retreat Contemporary accounts say the latter had a thousand Indians, besides his two hundred regulars

[9] We shall hear of Elliott again, at the river Raisin

gunboats and 11 or 12 pieces of ordnance, and landed about one mile and a half before we came to Fort Maggs * on the opposite shore. We then moved to nearly opposite the American fort, and began to erect batteries. Our preparations were soon discovered by the enemy, and they endeavoured to annoy us, by opening their batteries upon us, but we persevered until we had completed the works, with little or no loss, and we then returned the fire. We had a proof that our guns were doing execution, for one of our officers, with his glass, saw a man employed upon a building in the fort;[10] he supposed he was covering their magazine with turf. This officer pointed out the man to one of our gunners, who took an elevation and discharged the gun; the officer saw the man fall from the building.

Sergeant Smith and six of the light company (I being one of the number) were ordered to dig a place, for to lay a mortar, in front of the American fort. Sergeant Smith ordered me to go to the other battery and let the artillery officer know that the work was ready for the platform; and as I came up from the work I looked towards the fort and saw a smoke ascend, and then fell to the ground, when a ball passed over me and struck into the earth. I then went and gave the orders that Sergeant Smith sent me with. A few days after this, the grenadiers and light infantry were ordered back to the camp, and from thence crossed the river with a six-pounder and an howitzer, landed, and in the evening marched to within three or four hundred yards of the fort, and occupied a ravine where the enemy's guns could not bear on us, and by the morning made platforms for the gun and howitzer and commenced a fire upon the fort. Here we remained some days, and at night

* Fort Maggs is a strong fortification on the American side of the river. (*Byfield's Note*)

[10] Fort Meigs was built by Lieutenant-colonel E D Wood, of the Engineers, who was killed at the sortie from Fort Erie, in 1814, and whose monument, erected by his comrade, General Jacob Brown, is at West Point, N. Y.

sentries were posted in the woods, about 30 or 40 yards from the fort.

While lying in the ravine one day, I went up to look round, when a ball came near my head and struck a tree. I then looked round and saw an artilleryman shaving his comrade; the ball rebounded from the tree and struck the man that was shaved, in his head. He died in the evening of the same day, and left a wife and three children to mourn his melancholy fate.

One night, as I was on sentry, I heard a person coming through the woods. He accosted me and gave me to understand that the Americans were coming down on the other side of the river. When I went off sentry I acquainted the captain with what the Indian had said, who treated it very lightly; but about ten o'clock the next morning we heard a great noise and firing from the other side of the river.[11] On looking towards our batteries we were surprised to see our colours down; 1300 of the enemy's troops had come down and got possession of the batteries, with all the ordnance, &c. We then received orders to recross the river, and I and one of my comrades had orders to take a box of ammunition and throw it into a creek, to prevent its coming into the hands of the enemy. By the time we had done this the enemy had marched out of the forts, when my comrade said to me, "We can stop here, we have no need to go back to the fight": but I replied, "What, see your comrades fighting and not go back to help them? If you don't go back I will shoot you." I hastened back, but cannot tell how he acted. When I joined them they were rallying for the charge. We charged them close under the fort, but were obliged to retreat because of their great guns, and were ordered to make the best of our way to the boats, to cross the river. Several of the officers and men were taken prisoners. After crossing the river we had orders to march towards the batteries as quickly as possible. When ad-

[11] This was May 4, 1813.

vanced about half a mile we met a party of our men with a considerable number of the Americans (prisoners) and were informed that, on news being received at the camp that the enemy had taken possession of the batteries, the whole force were ordered under arms and marched for the batteries. Sergeant-Major Keynes with 12 men advanced in front, and when they came in sight of the enemy they commenced firing. The Sergeant-Major was soon wounded in one of his arms, and lost several of his men, but that did not stop them, they were bold and courageous. The main force was not far behind and very soon the fight became general and continued about twenty minutes, when the Americans surrendered, but some of them escaped to the woods.

We passed our men and the prisoners, and came to the batteries. The light infantry and a party of Indians received orders to go through the woods in search of those who had escaped. I witnessed several affecting scenes in this pursuit. I saw one of our men and one of the enemy lying dead near together. I saw another of the enemy that the Indians had met with and scalped, lying in a miserable plight and begging for water; while covering over his head with boughs, to screen it from the heat of the sun, a party of the Indians came up and found fault with us for shewing any lenity to the dying man; and one of them instantly despatched him with his tomahawk.[12] We took several prisoners in the woods and marched them to the camp. In this affair a considerable number on both sides were killed and wounded. The prisoners being secured and the detached men being come in, the Indians, who had lost many of their companions, began to manifest a disposition to be revenged on the prisoners, and actually fired amongst them and killed one of our men [13] who opposed them in their cruel intentions.

[12] This was very likely Colonel William Dudley, of Kentucky

[13] An old and excellent soldier, Russell, of the 41st., was killed while endeavoring to wrest a victim from the grasp of his assailant —Richardson *War of 1812.*

Our officers interfered, and prevailed upon Captain Elliott [14] and some of their chiefs, to put a stop to their cruel proceedings. The prisoners were then put on board the boats for safety, and put out into the stream. The flank companies were ordered back to the batteries, where we encamped. The same evening we heard that the American general had agreed to surrender Fort Maggs; and the next morning we were ordered back to the camp, and from thence we crossed the river with a flag of truce, under the command of General Proctor. General Harris * came from the fort with his attendants, and met our general on the beach, who told him he was come to receive the fort, according to his proposal. The American general said he should not surrender. General Proctor replied, "What, not fulfill your own agreement?—that would be a violation of the honours of war," or words to that effect. He said he should not give up, for he knew his (General Proctor's) strength was far less than his own; and further, that he knew his strength as well as he himself did. He was willing to exchange prisoners, and when that was effected, if they were not away in two hours he would open his batteries upon them. It was thought that the American general gained his information respecting our strength from four men who deserted from us the preceding night. We exchanged prisoners and recrossed the river. We then embarked the ordnance, &c, went on board the boats with the remaining prisoners, and sailed for Malden. The Enemy opened their guns upon us from the fort, but we were nearly clear of them, and sustained no loss. When we arrived at Malden we were employed when off duty, under the direction of engineers, in strengthening and throwing up works. While here, one day while on duty a sentinel was wanted on board a vessel, and I was sent. (I relate this circum-

[14] Lossing *(Field Book War of 1812)*, says Elliott was an uncle of two American officers Captain Elliott of the 19th Infantry, and Captain Jesse Elliott, of the Navy, then on duty with the Lake Erie fleet.

* William Henry Harrison

stance to shew something of the cruelty of the native Indians, when they have it in their power.) When I got on board the vessel, a person came from below, and was put in my charge; as we were walking the deck I entered into conversation with him, and as near as I can recollect, he related the following sad tale to me. I thought it deserved credit, for his feelings were much excited and the tears flowed freely and plentifully. He said he had a small fortified place, where he and others defended their property; if I remember right he said they were traders: "A party of Indians surrounded our place and told us that the British troops were near, and would undoubtedly destroy us and take away our property; but if we would admit them they would protect us and our property. Thinking that this re-enforcement would be the means of preserving myself, my family and my property, I consented and gave them possession; when they began the work of destruction. They first killed my associates and then cruelly murdered my children. Not satisfied with this they took my wife, who was in a forward state of pregnancy, and murdered her before my face; they then ripped her up and exposed the unborn infant, after which they took me off a prisoner." This was a very affecting relation; for hard and unfeeling as I then was, I could not help shedding tears on hearing it and seeing the distressed state of him who related it.

Some time after this we were informed that the Enemy were at the river Reasin.† Orders were given to cross the river St. Lawrence. We landed at a place called Brown's Town [15] and then proceeded for the river Reasin, with about 500 of our troops and a few Indians. We had to contend with about 1400 of the Enemy, under the command of General Winchester. When within about two miles of the Enemy we encamped for part of the night. Early in the morning we proceeded to meet them, and under cover of a

† Raisin.

[15] Michigan.

wood we approached near to them unperceived; we formed the line and had a view of them as they surrounded their fires. While we were forming the Indians marched so as to get round their right flank. We had six field-pieces, which led on in front of the line. We were then discovered by one of their sentries, who challenged and discharged his piece, which killed one of our grenadiers; we then gave three cheers and the Indians followed with a war-whoop; the fight then commenced very warmly. It was on the 22d day of January, 1813. Before daylight we had charged them several times, thinking that we were close upon their line, but our men were so cut up that after every attempt we were obliged to retreat to the covert of a rising piece of ground, with considerable loss. The men at the three guns[16], in our front of the line, were all killed or wounded, with the exception of one man. One of our lieutenants (Clemon[17]) received three or four wounds by musket balls, and a field-officer, I think a lieutenant-colonel, fell, having received several shots, but (as he) was not killed four of our men advanced to defend him, one of whom took him up and carried him into the rear. As the day approached we discovered that what had supposed to have been the Enemy's line was a made fence, behind which they were sheltered, with holes in it through which they fired at us. About this time my comrade on my left hand was killed. It being now light, I saw a man come from the fence, when I said to my comrade "There is a man, I'll have a shot at him." Just as I had said these words and pulled my trigger, I received a ball under my left ear, and fell immediately; in falling I cut my comrade's leg with my bayonet. He exclaimed "Byfield is dead"—to which I replied "I believe I be," and I thought to myself "Is this death, or how men do die?" As soon as I had recovered, so as to raise my head from the ground,

[16] So in the original, though on the preceding page he says six.

[17] The British Army List gives the names of James Clemens and John William Clemon, as lieutenants of the 41st.

I crept away upon my hands and knees and saw a sergeant in the rear who said, "Byfield, shall I take you to the doctor?" I said "Never mind me, go and help the men." I got to the place where the doctor was, who, when it came to my turn to be dressed, put a plaister to my neck and ordered me to go to a barn which was appointed for the reception of the wounded. As I was going the blood flowed so freely as to force off the plaister. I now saw a man between the woods, and asked him what he did there. He told me he was wounded in his leg. I observed to him that if I had not been worse that he was I should be back, helping the men. I then asked him to give me a pocket-handkerchief, to tie round my neck to stop the blood. He replied "I have not got one." I said "If I do not get something I shall bleed to death." He immediately tore off the tail of his shirt and wound it round my neck. I then got to the barn, and laid down with my fellow sufferers. I had not been there long before the doctor came and said "My dear fellows, you that can had better get away, for our men are terribly cut up and I fear we shall all be taken." He rode away, but soon returned saying, "My dear fellows, we have taken all of them prisoners"—at which news I exclaimed (being quite overjoyed), "I don't mind about my wound, since that is the case." While in the barn I was much affected by seeing and hearing a lad about 11 or 12 years of age, who was wounded in one of his knees. The little fellow's cries, from the pain of his wound, his crying after his dear mother, and saying that he should die, were so affecting that it was not soon forgotten by me. He was a midshipman belonging to one of the gunboats; I think his name was Dickenson. I understood that while we were engaged with the enemy the Indians pressed them on their right, and a part of the American force were sent to oppose them.

The Indians overpowered them and killed a considerable number (some of the Indians produced eight or nine scalps each). This no doubt was one of the principal causes of the enemy surrendering. There was a heavy loss of killed and wounded on each side. When we arrived at Malden there was a general muster of our men's wives, anxious to learn whose husbands were amongst the killed and wounded. The hospital would not contain the wounded, in consequence of which some of them were put into the barracks. I was among the latter The next morning I got my comrade to wash my neck and shoulder, and I told him there must be something the matter with my shoulder as I could scarcely lift my hand to my head. On examining my shoulder he thought he could feel a ball near the blade bone. I attended the doctor, and told him I had a job for him. On his examination he found that the ball which had entered my neck was lodged in my shoulder; he went to work and extracted it, and in about three weeks the wounds were nearly well, and I was able to attend to my duty.

The prisoners and wounded were brought to Malden, and after a short stay were sent down the country. Our light company received orders to march to Sandwich, where some of the company that had been detached joined us. We soon returned to Malden again and from thence with a large party of Indians went for Mawme Rapids, and landed about two miles from Fort Maggs. A plan was then formed to draw General Harris and his force from the fort. A body of the Indians was placed in the woods, and directed to keep firing as though two parties were engaged, in order to make the American general believe that we had fallen in with a re-inforcement which he was expecting, and endeavouring to prevent their joining him. We were in readiness to advance and cut off his retreat to the fort, if he came out. He came out from the fort, but the weather was tremendous, with thunder, lightning and hail. We supposed that they suspected or discovered the cheat, and returned immediately to the fort; as this project failed.[18] We returned down the river to Lake Huron, under orders for Fort

[18] This was July 25, 1813. General Green Clay was then in command.

St. Dresky.[19] We stopped at different places and went on shore, to see if we could obtain any information respecting the Enemy. At one place we discovered houses and plantations, but no inhabitants; but in one of the dwellings we found a dead body, partly consumed; we supposed this place had been depopulated by the Indians. At another place I and some of my comrades went some way into the woods, where I had a narrow escape from a rattlesnake. I did not see it at first. It was of great length and size. When I saw it I drew back (as) it appeared to be about to spring upon me; when one of my comrades shot it. We took it with us and the Indians begged it of us, saying that it was between nine and ten years old, and that some part of it would cure the bite of another.

We proceeded and went up the river St. Dresky, and disembarked on the beach. The following morning we marched for the fort. The Indians met with a man and the officers tried him very much to give some information respecting the enemy. He acted as though he was deaf and dumb, so that no information could be gained from him, neither by words nor signs. The gunboats went up the river, near to the fort, and we formed on a piece of ground at no great distance from it. The enemy commenced a fire upon the boats and us. The fire was returned from the boats. General Proctor sent Major Chambers with a flag of truce, and demanded the surrender of the fort, or he would blow them up. He was led into the fort blindfolded, and received an answer from the American general, for the commandant, that he would not surrender and that he was ready to be blown to hell at any minute. We then took up a position near the fort, where we were sheltered from their fire; and in the night made platforms for our guns. The following morning it was determined to storm. Our force was divided, and each party received orders which part of the fort to

[19] Lower Sandusky, now Fremont, Ohio. The post was Fort Stephenson; the commander, Major George Croghan, 17th Infantry

attack. It was thought at the distance we were at, that it would be possible to scale the fence. We advanced in file and formed near the ditch and found it much deeper than we had expected, and the fence much higher. The light company, and part of a battalion company were all that reached the works; the others were beaten back When the enemy found that the others had retreated, their main force was directed against us, and a dreadful scene ensued. Our men, generally, were determined, (but) I saw one of them turn round. His comrade observed it and said, if he did not face fire he would run his bayonet through him. We were exposed to the enemy's fire. My front-rank man, the sergeant on my right, Major Short[20] and Lieutenant Gordon, were killed. My left-hand man received six balls but recovered from his wounds. We that remained alive laid under the bank of the outer entrenchment. The officers and men in the inner ditch were exposed to a swivel gun,[21] and most of them were killed or wounded. I saw one of them come from thence into the ditch where I was, wounded in his mouth and the piece of lead lodged in it. We remained in the ditch until night, when we received orders to retreat. Before this I went down the ditch, amongst my dead and wounded comrades, to try to get some ammunition, as mine was expended. I said to one of my comrades, "Bill, how bee'st?" He said to me, "There is one of the Americans keeps firing upon us, out of one of those loop-holes." I asked him to tell me out of which of the holes he was firing, and I would have a shot at him. He told me, and I fired. I had scarcely fired when I saw my comrade fall back wounded. I stepped to him and said, "Bill, what's the matter?" He replied "They have shot me again." By this time the enemy

[20] William Charles Shortt and J G. Gordon They were buried at a point now near the N. E. corner of High and Market Streets, Fremont A piece of Shortt's sword-scabbard was found there in 1850, and is now owned by Mr. Sardis Birchard (*Lossing*).

[21] An iron six-pounder, still preserved at Fremont, and called *Good Bess*

had nearly ceased firing, and those of the men who could were getting out of the ditch as quickly as possible I do not believe there was either a commissioned or non-commissioned officer left in it, and our poor wounded men groaning and crying, saying " Now we have done the best we could, you are all going to leave us." This the American officer heard from the fort, and said, " I know your men are going away, but never mind, my brave fellows, when they are gone I will come out and take you in and use you well." I said to him, " Why don't you come out now, and we will fight you five to one." He answered, " No, I shall not, but when you are gone I shall come out and clear the ditch." I then said to one of my comrades, " Now I shall start," and ascended the works. Just as I had got to the top the flash of the guns caught my eye; I immediately fell on my face, when a shower of shot fell near me. I arose and hastened to one of our batteries, when jumping into it General Proctor said to me, " Where are all the rest of the men?" I said to him, " I don't think there are any more to come; they are all killed or wounded." He added, weeping, " Good God, what shall I do about the men?" This was in September, 1813.[22] We were then ordered to march to the boats. We went on board and proceeded down the river for Malden. Before we came to the lake we stopped and went ashore. Here one of my comrades, who was badly wounded, wanted to comply with nature's necessity, and asked me to carry him into the wood for that purpose. My feelings were so excited on account of the distressed state he was in, that I could not find courage enough, at the moment, to comply with his request; but one of my comrades took him up to carry him to the wood, and he died in his arms We dug a hole in the beach, and buried him; after which we arrived at Malden. The flank companies were then ordered to Sandwich. This is opposite Detroit When we took that place, in 1812, a circumstance occurred which I here refer to:

[22] A mistake—it was August 1st and 2nd.

An inhabitant of Detroit, a farmer who with his family were in comfortable circumstances, having a loom for weaving in their possession, sent to enquire if there were any weavers amongst us. I and one of my comrades being weavers, went to their house and lent them some assistance in putting the loom to work. They behaved very kindly to us. I visited them often afterwards, and they continued their kindness to me during our stay there. The mistress suggested to me that if I deserted and went into the States, I should do well. I told her I could not desert my colours, and that I hoped to see old England again.

Soon after we came to Sandwich I was one of a party that was sent across the river to Detroit for fuel. While they were getting it on board the boat I asked the sergeant to give me a few minutes' leave, to go and see my old acquaintance. I went to their former residence, but they were not there, the scene was changed. I found them in a cottage, reduced to a state of extreme poverty. The Indians had deprived them of all their property. The master was from home, the mistress said she was glad to see me, but had nothing to give me but a piece of bread. Having five shillings in my pocket, I gave it to her, and have never repented it since. I then took an affectionate leave of her and returned to the party. On recrossing the river with the fuel we were in danger of being sunk, by getting enclosed in a shoal of ice, but we were preserved, we got clear and landed about half a mile down the river. The flank companies were again ordered to Malden. A party from each company were now sent on board to do duty as marines, and the fleet sailed for Lake Huron, to attack the American fleet. The action commenced and we could hear the report of the guns and were expecting every hour to hear that our people were victorious; but contrary to our expectations news was brought that they were overpowered by numbers and every vessel taken.[23]

[23] This was Perry's victory on Lake Erie, not Huron, as Byfield has it.

Orders were then given to leave Malden and to take the ordnance and all that we could with us, but first to destroy the works, &c. In a few days' march we came to 24-mile Bush (or Moravian Town[24]) and were informed that the American general was pursuing us with three times our number, or more; and instead of using every effort to keep ahead of the enemy until we were re-inforced, were detained in taking forward the general's baggage, &c. It was said that the Indians were inclined to make a stand and endeavour to defeat the Enemy, in order to keep possession of the upper country. The Americans gained upon us, and the Indians brought in some of their advance (prisoners). A party was sent back to destroy a bridge, in order to check the enemy; while in the act they were surrounded and taken prisoners.[25] Thus situated we prepared to meet them in the best manner that we could. The light company and the Indians were placed on the right, to face the Kentucky riflemen.[26] We were thus formed, in a wood, when the enemy came within 20 or 30 yards of us and sounded the bugle, to advance and attack. The attack commenced on the right, with the Indians, and very soon became general through the line. After exchanging a few shots our men gave way. I was in the act of retreating, when one of our sergeants exclaimed, "For God's sake, men, stand and fight!" I stood by him and fired one shot, but the line was broken and the men were retreating. I then made my escape farther into the wood, where I met with some of the Indians, who said that they had beaten back the enemy on the right, but that their prophet was killed, and they then retreated. Moravian Town was not far from us, and the Indians wanted to know whether it was in the possession of the enemy or not. They made for this place, placing me in front,

[24]The town of the Moravian or Christian Indians, not far from the battle-field. They were mostly of the Delaware tribe.

[25] A squad of eleven privates and a lieutenant of the dragoons

[26] This was the battle of the Thames, October 5, 1813.

and their interpreter asked me, in case I should hear the voice of any one there, whether I should know it to be an Englishman's or an American's. I said I should. When near the outside of the wood I heard a voice saying, "Come on, my boys," in a dialect which I knew to be American. I communicated the same to the interpreter, and finding that we were discovered by the enemy, the Indians turned round and made their way through the woods as fast as possible. I followed after as quickly as I could. After awhile they slackened their pace and I overtook them; we went forward until night came on, when the Indians halted and formed around me, they seemed to be holding a consultation, I supposed it was to decide how I should be disposed of. In this solitary place and surrounded by savages, whose cruelties I was somewhat acquainted with, I had but little hope at the moment, of ever getting out of the woods. My feelings on this occasion may be more readily conceived than expressed. After a short time they went on in Indian file, and I followed until we discovered a light: I was then ordered to go on in front to ascertain what light it was. I found an old Indian and a little boy, the old man being too far advanced in age to go to war. They then came on, had some conversation and stopped for the night. I wanted to gain their friendship if I could, and having some tobacco in my haversack I distributed it amongst them, and then laid down. After passing the night there we proceeded through the woods, and after some time discovered some cattle feeding. As we advanced we came to an Indian camp, and after some conversation between my companions and them, one of the females gave me some victuals and spoke to me in broken English. I understood that she invited me to go with them, that is, with their tribe. I accepted the invitation. The interpreter hearing it, called me aside and asked what I had been saying. I told him. He then told me that if I went with them I should go into the back settlements, and perhaps never come out of the woods again. This caused me to change my mind. I told the interpreter that I wanted to find out some road or river, thinking that I should then find my way to some house or place. He then told me that I had better go with him, as he should be in Quebec some time in the following month.

The interpreter and three of the Indians then left the others, and I went on with them. We had not travelled far when I observed one of the Indians give the interpreter a pair of moccasons for the feet. I then thought that the interpreter had sold me for a pair of shoes, and I showed some reluctance to go forward. He asked me why I did not go on. I said that I should not, without him. He replied, "You are afraid." I answered, "I am not." (I really was afraid, but did not want him to know it.) We proceeded through the woods until the sun had nearly set I thought we were drawing near some road (so) I mended my pace, and was getting in front of them, when one of the Indians tapped me on the head, and said that if I did not keep further back he would take that off. We went a little farther and picked up a pompion; in a short time after I discovered one of my comrades. This was the best sight I had seen in some time, and my fears and suspicions in a great measure vanished. He had been wandering about, going he knew not where, and no doubt was as glad to see me as I was to see him. Soon after this we came in sight of a public road, and by the roadside we found some flour, some potatoes and a kettle. We returned with the Indians into the wood and cooked it; we made a division of it and found it very refreshing, being so much needed. We stopped in the wood that night; there was a heavy fall of rain, which made it very uncomfortable. The next morning we crossed the road and went into the woods on the other side; we forded several rivers, and in the evening came to an Indian village. We were invited to one of the huts, and the head of the family was very kind; he killed a pig and dressed it, boiled some Indian corn and made soup, and entertained the whole of us in a very friendly manner. We slept there that night, and in the morning I and my companion took leave of the old man and our traveling companions, who directed us towards Oxford. The same day we fell in with a party of our men, who had charge of the general's baggage. We stopped with them that night; in the morning I found that they were making too free with what they had in charge. I was afraid of the consequences and said to my comrade, "Let us push forward," but he was inclined to stay, and I went on without him. I was ill-prepared for marching, my shoes being entirely worn out; but before night I fell in with a large party of our men who had escaped, under the command of Captain Bullock,[27] of the grenadier company. He enquired how I had escaped. I related to him the particulars of what I had passed through. This party proceeded to Oxford, and from thence to the Cross Roads, where we remained several months.

From thence we marched to Burlington Heights barracks, and after a few days, to Fort George, the Americans having left it. Our flank companies, with the 100th regiment, were ordered to attack Fort Niagara. The 100th regiment was at Queen's Town. We marched to that place and joined them, and from thence crossed the river St. Lawrence and landed about four or five miles above Niagara. Generals Drummond [28] and Ryal [29] were with us. Arrangements being made, we moved off for the fort; the 100th regiment was in front. On the way we surprised a guard at Young's Town; we took them prisoners and obtained the countersign, but a man made a signal, by discharging a rocket, we supposed to alarm the fort; it had no effect, and the man was killed. We advanced quietly, and a party under the command of a sergeant went in front. When he came near the outer sentry, at the entrance to the fort, he was challenged. He gave the countersign, seized the sentinel and threatened him with immediate death if he made any

[27] Captain Richard Bullock, of the 41st

[28] Sir Gordon Drummond

[29] General Sir Phineas Riall (1772-1854.)

noise. He then proceeded to the gate and was challenged by the sentry inside. He gave the countersign and gained admittance, but the sentry cried out, "The British—turn out the guard!" Our force was fully prepared, and in a very short time we had possession of the fort, with very little loss—December 19th, 1813. The 100th regiment was left in the fort, and we were ordered to Lewis Town, which place was occupied by a small party of the enemy, but before we got there they had quitted the station, leaving one piece of ordnance. Here we were re-inforced by a party of the 1st (Royals) from Queen's Town; we were then ordered for Slustra.[30] We were a little alarmed in the evening before we started; I was on sentry, and heard something like the movement of troops. It proved to be a party of Indians, bringing two men belonging to the Royals, who they thought were about to desert. We proceeded the same night, for Slustra (I was on the advance, with a sergeant's party) and when within about one mile and a half of it we fell in with an American guard. The sentinel challenged, and attempted to fire, but his piece missed fire. We forced our way into the guard-room, where they were all in confusion; I seized one of them in a sailor's dress, and threatened to kill him if he made any resistance. We made eight of them prisoners, the others escaped. Our main force went on, and I, with some others, followed with the prisoners. We had not marched far before we came to two roads; we took the wrong one. Soon after we heard some person coming behind. Not having a non-commissioned officer with us, I said to one of my comrades, "Go back, there is somebody coming," but he refused. I then said, "Take care of the prisoners, and I will go back." I had not gone far when I saw a man, I challenged and he answered, "A friend." I asked him what he belonged to—he said, "The Americans." I ordered him to stand fast, or I would blow his brains out. He replied, "I am a prisoner." I took hold of him. He then said, "You are one of the men who came into the house just now. One of

[30] Schlosser.

you has got my boots; I am the officer of the guard." I told him that I had a pair of shoes in my knapsack, and that he might have them if he would. He said that if he put them on his feet would be frost-bitten—December 22nd, 1813. I offered him some rum. He said he did not expect to be so treated if he was taken a prisoner, and wept, begging that I would not let him fall into the hands of the Indians. I told him that if he behaved himself no one should hurt him.

We now halted, thinking to remain until daylight, in order to ascertain the right road; we again heard some one coming. I went back some distance and challenged. I was answered, "A friend." I asked him what he belonged to; he replied "The British." I asked him what regiment he belonged to; he replied, "The militia." Not being satisfied with his answers, I drew near to him and took his arms and ammunition from him. A short time after we saw another man, with polished arms, by which I knew that he must be one of our men. I said to him, "You villain, what business have you got here?" He asked me who I was, and said he was as good a soldier as I was, and challenged me to fight. One of our men (a jocular fellow) said to him, "You do not know who you are talking to, he is an officer and will have you shot to-morrow." I had a beaver hat on, and a silk handkerchief round my neck (I had lost my cap in the tussle at the guard-room, and found the hat; and was allowed to wear a handkerchief, on account of the wound in my neck). From this the fellow thought that there was some truth in what was said, and begged that I would not report him; but before daylight he thought proper to depart. He belonged to the Royals.

When the morning came, we proceeded and soon came into the right road. We found that our men had got possession of Slustra, which was a mill and a place for public stores. The guard made some resistance, and the officer commanding it was killed.

I saw him lying dead and asked the officer (my prisoner) if he knew him. He said that he was a dear friend of his, wept over him, and said that he had been on parole three times. I then gave up the prisoners, and was put on guard to prevent the men from making free with the liquors &c. in the stores. Orders were then given to destroy the stores, and to burn the buildings; some of the provisions were thrown into the river. When this work of destruction was completed we returned to Lewis Town. Two circumstances happened here of a very serious nature. One of our men went into the woods and was murdered by an Indian. We manifested much displeasure respecting it. The tribe, to make an atonement for this act, caused the murderer to be killed, and exposed in the public road for some days. We were ordered under arms one night, when one of our men by his carelessness caused his piece to explode, and the contents passed through his right-hand man, and killed him.

From Lewis Town we crossed the river for Queen's Town—December 22nd, 1813. We marched up the lines, to cross over again in order to attack Black Rock, and were re-inforced on the way by men from the Royals and 8th regiment. Our force was then divided. The Royals went above Fort Erie, to cross the river above Black Rock; the remainder was to cross below Fort Erie, so as to land below Black Rock Fort Erie is nearly opposite Black Rock, on the opposite side of the river. We effected our landing according to orders. The first that landed surprised a guard commanded by a Major Cotton[30a] and took them prisoners. The line was then formed and (we) had orders to remain still until morning, if nothing happened and then to advance, on the firing of a gun. We had not been there long when a person came mounted, within 20 yards of our line, and exclaimed, "Damn you, Major Cotton, where are you, and the British landing?" General Ryal, being not far from him said, "I pray, Sir, who are you?"

[30a] Probably Salmon C. Cotton, captain 26th Infantry.

The other replied by asking the same question. The former answered, "I am a British general," and challenged him. The other said, "I am an American general." General Ryal then said, "If you are a man and a soldier, stand before me." He instantly turned his horse and rode off in great haste. The Royals, in crossing the river, were carried by the violence of the stream so far down the river as to be exposed to the enemy's batteries, and suffered much, but they effected a landing. Some time after this the Americans came out of the town, and formed. We laid close and quiet according to order, and heard the American general say, "Make ready, present, blaze." Their shot took no effect upon us. We arose, returned the fire, and lay down again. As they did not fire again we concluded that they had retreated.

We remained in our position until the gun fired, when we faced to the right, and having gained some ground to the right, turned off the left by sections, and advanced until we came near to the entrance of the town, where we formed the line on the first section. They fired upon us as we were forming and we returned it as fast as the sections came into line. The enemy soon began to give way. There was a heavy fire kept up from a large building. A party of our men advanced, and stopped the firing by taking possession of the building. We now discovered that the Royals were exposed to their batteries, being carried further down the river than was intended. We then directed our fire upon the men that were working the battery guns. About this time the enemy sent a party into the wood, to flank us on the left; but they were received by a party of our Indians stationed there for that purpose, and were beaten back with loss. They made an attempt to turn one of their battery guns upon us, but could not succeed. As many of the Royals as survived, about this time effected a landing. We now pressed the enemy very closely, and they began to retreat for Buffaloe. We got possession of Black Rock and the batteries, and pursued them to Buffaloe. I saw one of the Royals, with blood flowing very freely from his face; I said to him, "You are wounded, you had better go back." He replied, "No, lad, I'll pay some of them first." The enemy made but a short stay at Buffaloe. They gave us a shot from a mounted gun, and retreated. We took possession of the place, being apprehensive that the enemy would get re-inforcements and return upon us. Orders were given to destroy both places by burning; no dwelling was to be spared except one, where the dead body of a child laid, who had been shot in the street; this was in compassion towards the sorrowful mother. We stopped until the evening, refreshing ourselves and burying the dead, and then recrossed the river and marched down the lines to Fort George. At this place my brother met with an accident which cost him his life.

When our company was at this place before the taking of Detroit, we were 110 strong, but now reduced to 15 men only fit for duty; some of them had been wounded, myself for one. The other part of the company, both officers, non-commissioned officers and privates, were either killed, wounded or taken prisoners.

We marched from Fort George to York, where the second battalion joined us, July 25th, 1814.

Our company, now filled up, was ordered, under the command of Captain Glue,[30] to Point Frederick, Kingston, supposing that the Americans would cross from Sacket's Harbour, and attack it. We remained here until the weather broke up, and then returned to York again.

About this time, the man who messed the officers complained that owing to the high price of provisions he could not continue to do it, without permission to keep a canteen, and to be allowed a man to assist him. Permission being granted, he requested to have me; as I belonged to the light company he was at first denied, but it was afterwards granted, with an order that whenever the com-

[30] John Berry Glew.

pany was wanted for any particular duty I was to attend. While at York I went into the hospital to see the wounded. One of the 8th regiment, who had lost a leg, said, "That's the man that saved my life," and related how, saying that when he was knocked down I had pulled him behind a tree, to shelter him from the enemy's fire. I recalled the circumstance; he was very kind to me during our stay together.

Our regiment now received orders for Fort Niagara, to relieve the 100th regiment. While here we were expecting the enemy, and were often under arms all night and the guns all loaded, to receive them if they attempted to storm. The light company was repeatedly sent across the river to Fort George as there was a force of the enemy in that quarter. The enemy made their appearance, but the forts were opened upon them and they went back. The flank companies were then ordered to Lewis Town, information having been received that the enemy were in that neighbourhood. A field-piece accompanied us, and the light company was extended into the wood, on the side of the road, to prevent us from being surprised from thence. We found much obstruction, the enemy having blocked the way with a large quantity of brushwood. When we came near Lewis Town we got sight of a party of the enemy, encamped. When they saw us they went off in quick time and left the camp, and their provisions partly dressed. We followed them some distance, but they did not stop to face us and we returned. At this time [31] the British on the other side of the river were engaged with the enemy, at Lundie's Lane. We could hear the report of their great guns. Our captain informed us that he had received orders to cross the river to assist them; and the grenadiers, with the field-piece, were to return to Niagara. We crossed and landed at Queen's Town. It was at this place that the much-lamented veteran, General Brock, received his death wound by a

[31] July 25, 1814

shot from an American rifleman. We moved from this place in quick time, for about seven miles, and waited for orders near Lundie's Lane. A noggin of rum was given to each man. We then moved on for the field of action. We had a guide with us, and when we came near the field our captain was called upon by name, in a loud voice, to form on the left of the speaker. It being night we could not discover what regiment it was. The guide positively asserted that it was one of the enemy. Our bugle then sounded, for the company to drop. A volley was then fired upon us which killed two corporals and wounded a sergeant and several of the men. The company then arose, fired and charged. The enemy quitted their position; we followed and took three field-pieces. In the morning we collected the wounded and received orders to burn the dead. One of the Indians persisted on throwing one of the wounded Americans on the fire while living, although prevented several times; one of our men shot him and he was burned himself. At this fight General Ryal was wounded, and himself and his orderly (one of the 19th dragoons) were taken prisoners. We were now ordered to join the regiment at Niagara; but before we marched General Drummond personally thanked us for our conduct in the fight. The whole of the army were thanked in public orders, namely the Royals, 8th, 49th, 89th and 103d regiments. The 89th suffered severely in this engagement.

We joined our regiment at Niagara, and in a short time part of the regiment, including the light company, was ordered to cross the river to Fort George, and from thence towards Fort Erie. In going up the lines we fell in with our main force. We were expecting to storm Fort Erie, when orders were given for the 41st and part of the 104th, with a rocket party under the command of Captain Perry, to cross the river below Black Rock. While on the water we heard firing in the direction of Black Rock. We landed [32]

[32] August 3, 1814

and advanced towards it. When we were here last there was a bridge between us and the town, over a small creek, but the enemy had destroyed it, and on the inner bank they had thrown up breastworks. They commenced firing upon us, we advanced, thinking to charge, when we discovered that the bridge was gone. We instantly retreated, and remained until daylight, when a party was ordered to erect a temporary bridge across the creek, and our company and the rocket company were to cover them. We stood some time and some of our shot took effect. We saw one of the enemy fall, who was daring enough to get upon their works. About this time I received a musket ball through my left arm, below the elbow. I went into the rear. One of my comrades, seeing that I was badly wounded, cut my belts from me and let them drop. I walked to the doctor, and desired him to take my arm off. He said it might be cured without it, and ordered me down to a boat, saying that the wounded men were to cross the river and they (the doctors) would soon follow. The party failed in erecting the bridge, and retreated with loss. When on the other side of the river, the wounded were put into a house and the doctors soon came. They examined my arm, and made preparations for amputation; but after a further consultation they told me that although I was rendered unfit for further service, yet if the wound could be healed it would be better for my hand to remain on, if it was not much use to me, and that it had better be first tried. I was then sent to my regiment at Niagara.

After a few days our doctor informed me that my arm must be taken off, as mortification had taken place. I consented, and asked one of my comrades who had lately gone through a like operation: "Bill, how is it to have the arm taken off?" He replied, "Thee woo't know, when it's done." They prepared to blind me, and had men to hold me, but I told them there was no need of that. The operation was tedious and painful, but I was enabled to bear it pretty well. I had it dressed, and went to bed. They brought me some mulled wine and I drank it. I was then informed that the orderly had thrown my hand to the dung heap. I arose, went to him, and felt a disposition to strike him. My hand was taken up and a few boards nailed together for a coffin, my hand was put into it and buried on the ramparts. The stump of my arm soon healed, and three days * after I was able to play a game of fives for a quart of rum; but before I left the fort a circumstance happened which I here relate. There was a sentry posted near the wood to prevent any of the men entering it, and we had to go near the sentry for water. One of the artillerymen went on pretence of fetching some water, and when the sentry's back was turned towards him he started into the wood for the purpose of deserting, and the sentry (one of the 41st) shot him. The ball entered his body and the wound proved mortal; he was brought into the barracks. His captain came into the barracks to see him. The dying man charged him with being the cause of what had happened. The captain left the room, and he died shortly after. My comrades, and the messman whom I had been serving, out of kindness and respect to me made a subscription of several pounds and gave it to me. As soon as the wounded men were somewhat recovered they were ordered from the different regiments to go on board the boats used on the river, to go to Kingston, and in going down the river we went on shore by night.

On board the boat I was in was a young man, a sailor, who had lost one of his arms near the shoulder. I felt a kind regard towards him, and we became comrades. He was going down the country to be cook on board a King's ship, the *St Lawrence,* 110 guns; he shared with me the gratuity my friends had bestowed upon me. From Kingston we proceeded to Montreal, and from thence to Quebec. One evening after going ashore, I took a walk

* Probably a misprint for "weeks."

alone a little way into the country and came near a large neat-looking house, and seeing a lad I asked who lived there; he replied, "A three-handed man." I said "That's the very man that I want to see, as I have but one hand; if he should be disposed to give me one of his, we shall have two apiece!" The lad said that by a "three-handed man" they meant that he was wealthy. After going a little farther I went into a farmhouse the inhabitants of which behaved very kindly to me, and the mistress made up a bed for me for the night. When I came to Quebec I met with some of my old comrades who had been wounded and taken prisoners. I was extremely glad to see them. They related the scenes and hardships they had passed through, and one of them said he was left amongst the dead (as) his wounds were considered incurable; but he begged them to attend to him for he thought he should recover. After remaining in that state four days before anything was done for him, they paid some attention to him. He was then in a great measure recovered, but not well. General Proctor being in Quebec I waited on him and asked him for a certificate for the capture of Detroit, which he freely gave me; and told me that he would give me such a recommendation that I need not fear but that a sufficient provision would be made for me. He asked me the particulars of the battle at Moravian Town. I told him all the particulars I knew. He further said that he was going to Montreal, and ordered me to call on him before he went or before he embarked for England. Some time after a woman told me that the general wanted me. I attended to the order immediately, but the woman had delayed delivering the message. The general was gone and I did not see him, neither have I had the satisfaction of seeing either of my officers since, although I have made many enquiries.

We now had orders to go on board the *Phoenix* transport and sailed for England. We had a tolerably good passage, but was a little alarmed one night, by a sudden squall of wind. The sails backed and we were near foundering, but in a short time the vessel righted and all was well. We landed in the Isle of Wight, and marched into Newport barracks December, 1814.

After examination we were sent to Chatham by water. Having been passed by the inspecting officer there I was sent to Chelsea. I appeared before the board and was ordered nine pence per day, pension.

My feelings were much excited that day, on learning that our bugle-horn man, who was a young soldier, who had been but in one action and had lost a forearm, about the same length as mine, was rewarded with one shilling per day. I must say that I felt very much dissatisfied with nine pence, and I made applications at different times to the Honourable Commissioners of Chelsea Hospital, to augment my pension, but without success. Hearing of a field-officer, residing in the neighbourhood of the town where I live, and that he was a soldier's friend, I made bold to wait upon him, and requested that he would be pleased to hear my case. He kindly condescended to comply with my request, and after hearing my statement he was of opinion that I was not remunerated for my services and loss. He very kindly said he would represent my case; and it was not merely a *promise,* he persevered until he had caused an addition to be made to my pension, of three pence per day. For which I very kindly thank him, and shall be ever bound gratefully to acknowledge his kindness to me. Being deprived of my trade in consequence of losing my arm in the service and having received several very severe wounds, it was with great difficulty I could support my wife and children in a respectable manner, my pension at that time being only ninepence per day.

One night I dreamt that I was working at my trade; and on awaking I related my dream to my wife and told her I could weave. She said, "Go to sleep, there was never such a thing known as a person having but one arm, to weave"; and on going to sleep a second time, I had the form of an instrument revealed to me, which would enable me to work at my trade. I awoke my wife and told her of the circumstance. I went to a blacksmith of the name of Court, and having drawn a design for him on a board, he made an instrument for me, similar to the pattern with the exception of some little alteration, which I thought was for the best, but which, on trial, I was obliged to alter to the shape I saw in my dream; and I am happy to say that I have been enabled to labour for my family and keep them comfortably, for nearly twenty years, in the employ of Edward Cooper, Esq., clothier, Staverton Works, near Bradford, Wilts.

The above is a true and correct account, as given by Shadrach Byfield, before me.

EDWARD COOPER.

January 1st, 1840.

I cannot but remark that it is evident in the foregoing relation that a kind Providence has preserved my life through the many dangers to which I have been exposed, and brought me back to my native home. And for what purpose? In order to manifest a further display of his goodness and mercy towards me, in convincing that I was a sinner and in high rebellion against Him who is my best friend and benefactor. A conviction of this has caused me to lay down my arms of rebellion, to sue for mercy, and to submit to his righteous sceptre. For the last twenty years I have been fighting under the banner of a Captain who has conquered every enemy and defeated every foe, to my immortal interest. Although I have to contend with a threefold enemy, namely the world, the flesh and the devil, and am the subject of many imperfections and rank myself among the vilest of the vile, yet I hope that my soul is founded on the Rock of Ages, against which the powers of hell shall never prevail. And when I shall have to encounter the last enemy, Death, although he will gain a victory over my mortal part, yet I hope that my immortal soul will be enabled to shout "Victory" through the blood of the Lamb; and be admitted into the society of the blessed, where I shall be beyond the gun-shot of my enemy and landed safely on the shores of eternal rest; *where peace reigns* and where war shall be known no more. Where a blessed eternity will be spent in adoration and praise to Him who has redeemed and saved me out of the hands of every enemy.

THE END

Milton Keynes UK
Ingram Content Group UK Ltd.
UKHW021437290424
441933UK00030B/310

9 781015 704817